Martha
Helps the Rebel

a story in play form
by Carole Charles
pictures by Bob Seible

 THE CHILD'S WORLD ELGIN, ILLINOIS 60120

On February 11, 1780, British General Clinton landed on John's Island, 30 miles south of Charleston, South Carolina. He began preparing his troops to march on Charleston. General Lincoln heard of this and gathered the American forces to defend the city. Soldiers and civilians alike worked feverishly to prepare Charleston for the attack.

By March 7, Clinton and his troops had arrived at Charleston, and by the end of April, Charleston was surrounded, its lines of supplies and ways of retreat cut off.

The soldiers in Charleston defended the city valiantly, but the overwhelming strength of the British made the situation hopeless. On May 11, 1780, General Lincoln was forced to surrender to the British.

The loss of Charleston was a great blow to the Americans, but they continued to fight the British on other fronts until they were ultimately victorious.

Library of Congress Cataloging in Publication Data

Charles, Carole, 1943-
  Martha Helps the Rebel.

  (Stories of the Revolution)
  SUMMARY: In 1780 a young girl helps an American soldier pursued by the British to escape.
  1. United States—History—Revolution, 1775-1783 —Juvenile drama. [1. United States—History—Revolution, 1775-1783—Drama.] 2. Plays I. Seible, Bob. II. Title.
PN6120.H5C48   [Fic]   75-33126
ISBN 0-913778-22-2

Distributed by Childrens Press, 1224 West Van Buren Street, Chicago, Illinois 60607

Martha
Helps the Rebel

While this play is fiction, there were American soldiers who crossed enemy lines in disguise in order to carry information. And, undoubtedly, there were civilians like Martha and her mother who helped them.

(Setting: South Carolina, 1780. From the back of their farmhouse, a mother and her ten-year-old daughter, Martha, watch three American soldiers walk through the nearby woods.)

Martha: Look at the soldiers, ma!

Mother: I see them, Martha. They must be coming from Charleston.

Martha: Are they American soldiers?

Mother: Yes.

Martha: I wish I were big enough to be a soldier like pa. I'd chase all the British soldiers right back to England! Would you like to be a soldier, ma?

Mother: *(musing)* Sometimes I would. But you and I need to take care of the farm until your pa comes home.

(Three American soldiers walking through the woods. British soldiers in hiding nearby.)

1st Am. Soldier: *(sings)* "Come all you brave soldiers, Both valiant and free, It's for independence, We all now agree."

2nd Am. Soldier: Hey, quiet down! Everyone in South Carolina can hear you.

1st Am. Soldier: Good! Then all the British soldiers in the colony will run at the sound of my voice. *(Sings the song again, just as loudly.)*

3rd Am. Soldier: Come on, quiet down. If any British soldiers have landed this far south, I'd like to hear them before they hear us.

1st Am. Soldier: Ah, there aren't any British around here.

3rd Am. Soldier: Maybe not. That's what we're supposed to find out.

(Woods. 1st Am. soldier whistling the tune from previous scene.)

2nd Am. Soldier: When we get back to Charleston, I'd like to...

(Interrupted by a musket shot, Whistling stops abruptly. 2nd Am. soldier yells and falls dead.)

3rd. Am. Soldier: British! Stay down!

(Shots fired from both sides.)

1st Am. Soldier: *(whispering)* Let's run for it. We'll never be able to hold them off here.

3rd Am. Soldier: All right...now!

(Musket shot strikes 3rd Am. soldier, who yells and falls.)

1st Am. Soldier: Oh, no! *(Fiercely, to himself)* I have
to get out of here!

*(Soldier exits, running, crouched. Sound of feet running,
crashing through low brush.
Muskets fire several more times.)*

(Woods. American soldier enters, running through low brush. About eight British soldiers pursue. American soldier exits on other side.)

1st Br. Soldier: Let's get him!

2nd Br. Soldier: *(panting heavily)* I can hardly run with this heavy pack.

3rd Br. Soldier: *(also panting)* Hey, just a minute. Slow down. Listen, he can outrun us easily. We're wearing winter uniforms and carrying packs. All the American has to carry is a musket.

1st Br. Soldier: But we have to stop him before he reaches Charleston. The American army must not know our position or strength.

3rd Br. Soldier: *(still breathing heavily)* I know. So let's outsmart that American soldier. Hide the packs somewhere in the bushes. Then spread out and we'll search the ways to Charleston. He'll have to stop for food and water, perhaps for rest. If we move quickly, we'll find him.

(Martha grooms a riding horse. Mother enters. Mother and Martha see the American soldier running through the woods as if pursued.)

Martha: Ma, look!

Mother: I see. Martha, ride old Jonathan as fast as you can to that soldier. Bring him back by the stream bed so no one will see him. I'll wait in the kitchen.

Martha: What if there are British soldiers right behind him?

Mother: You said you wanted to fight. This is your chance. Hurry, before it's too late.

(Martha and horse exit. Sound of hoofbeats.)

(Kitchen. Mother is lowering a quilting frame from the ceiling. Frame has a nearly completed quilt attached. Soldier and Martha enter from side. Soldier appears haggard, exhausted.)

Mother: Martha, go back outside and ride old Jonathan hard around the pasture, as though you were exercising him. If anyone comes, I don't want a panting horse tied to my front porch.

Martha: Yes, ma. *(Exits.)*

Soldier: Ma'am, I...

Mother: *(interrupting)* We can talk later. Right now I want you up on those rafters, right over the spot where the quilting frame will be.

Soldier: Up there? But...

Mother: *(interrupting)* Soldier, if you want to live, you'd better get up on those rafters, and fast!

(American soldier balanced on the rafters. Mother raising the quilting frame. British soldiers can be seen through a window, approaching the house from the woods.)

Am. Soldier: Ma'am, you don't know how much I appreciate your help.

Mother: *(speaking as she raises the frame)* It's all right. My husband is a soldier with the Continental Army too. Maybe someone will help him one day.

Am. Soldier: I'm very grateful for...

Mother: *(interrupting)* Hush! *(whispering)* Soldiers coming! Don't make a sound!

(Loud knocks on the door.)

Br. Soldier: *(from outside)* Open up! *(More loud knocks.)* Open up, I say!

(Kitchen. American soldier completely hidden from view by quilt and frame. Mother has lifted hot skillet off fireplace in pretense of busyness. Loud knocks continue.)

Mother: Just a minute!

(More loud knocks. British soldiers push open the door and enter the kitchen.)

Br. Soldier: Sorry, ma'am. We're looking for someone.

Mother: (indigant) You might have waited until I opened the door!

(Soldiers begin searching the house.)

Mother: What are you doing!

Br. Soldier: Looking for someone, like I said. Arnold, you keep watch outside. Two of you search the barn and grounds. The rest of you search every inch of this house.

Mother: You have no right to search my house!

Br. Soldier: You have nothing to be afraid of, ma'am, (threateningly) unless we find an American soldier here.

(Kitchen. Mother seated. British soldiers still searching. Martha comes running in.)

      Martha: Ma! What are they doing?

      Mother: They're just looking for someone, Martha.

  Br. Soldier: Where have you been, little girl?

      Martha: *(defiant)* My name is Martha, not "little girl"! I've been out riding my horse.

  Br. Soldier: *(quiet but threatening)* You wouldn't have been hiding an American soldier somewhere, would you?

      Martha: *(still defiant)* I told you, I was riding my horse.

Mother: Martha, come sit down with me. They'll be leaving soon.

Martha: *(through clenched teeth)* I hope so!

(Kitchen. American soldier climbing down from rafters. Twilight.)

Mother: It's safe now. The British have gone.

Soldier: Thank you. I'm very grateful. *(Thoughtful)* Do you know if there are many British around?

Mother: We haven't seen British soldiers for several months, until today.

Martha: *(excited)* I'll bet there are thousands of British just over the hill, ready to attack Charleston!

Soldier: *(laughing gently)* Well, perhaps. But we rather expect an attack from the sea. That's how they attacked at the beginning of the war.

Martha: Maybe they're trying to trick you! You should go look for yourself. I'll bet there are thousands of British over there, just polishing their muskets and laughing.

Soldier: *(slowly)* That is possible. Perhaps I should take a look as soon as it's dark.

(Early morning, outside the farmhouse. Mother milking a cow. Martha enters, carrying a basket of eggs. Soldier rushes onstage.)

Soldier: You were right, Martha! The British are landing along the coast. It looks as though they are preparing to march on Charleston.

Mother: *(very nervous)* Keep your voice down! The British came back again last night. They're still looking for you, and for any other American soldiers. All the roads are guarded.

Soldier: And I know why! Most of our troops in Charleston are guarding the coast. If the British attack from the south, they will meet almost no resistance.

Martha: You'll have to tell them! You'll have to get through!

Mother: But how? It would be easier for...for this cow to pass the British. An American soldier couldn't make it!

Martha: I have an idea!

(Martha, mother, and soldier taking clothes out of a chest. Soldier half dressed as an old farmer.)

Mother: Pa won't mind our giving these clothes to you. They just might help you get past the British.

Martha: You really look like a farmer! *(Laughs with delight.)*

Soldier: Martha, you had a good idea. And making me look so old is the best part of the disguise.

(Dirt road. British soldiers standing guard, blocking road. American soldier disguised as old farmer enters, accompanied by Martha, who leads a milk cow.)

"Farmer": Afternoon, gentlemen.

1st Br. Soldier: Hold on, old man. Where are you taking the cow?

"Farmer": Yonder, to the next town. The little girl has a cousin who wants to buy her milk cow.

1st Br. Soldier: She looks old enough to take an old gentle cow to the next town by herself. Why are you going, mister?

Martha: I'll tell you why. Because I'm afraid to go by myself, that's why. I've never seen so many soldiers around here. I...I'm just afraid.

2nd Br. Soldier: Ah, let them go. You're scaring the little girl. The old man is harmless.

"Farmer": (moving on) Afternoon, gentlemen.

(American soldier disguised as farmer and Martha walk off with cow. British soldiers still stand guard. British troops approach in formation from south.)

    1st Br. Soldier: I wish we knew what happened to that American soldier. If he makes it to Charleston, he'll tell them all about us.

"Farmer", offstage: *(sung in cracked old man's voice)*
      "Come all you brave soldiers, Both valiant and free, It's for independence, We all now agree."

On Independence

Folk tune

Jonathan Mitchell Sewall

Come all you brave sol-diers, both val-iant and free, It's for in-de-pen-dence, we all now a-gree; Let us gird on our swords and pre-pare to de-fend Our li-ber-ty, pro-per-ty, our-selves and our friends.

812
CHA

Charles, Carole. 6790
C. 2

Martha helps the
rebel.

DATE DUE	BORROWER'S NAME	ROOM NO.
11/17		
MAY 2	Oliver	3C

5.74
$5.36

6790
C. 2

812
CHA

Charles, Carole.

Martha helps the
rebel.